Ahmed is Home

J. Malcolm Garcia

A version of Ahmed Is Home
appeared in
The Missouri Review Winter 2025

Fomite
Burlingon, VT
fomitepress.com

One afternoon, a photo on Instagram caught my attention. It showed a woman sitting on a bench. She wore dark sunglasses, a blue plaid shirt and blue jeans, and creased, black boots. A multicolored bandanna covered her head, and strands of long gray hair fell to her shoulders. She was holding a bottle of water and staring off to her left. Her lined face suggested that she had covered many miles and had seen enough of life for it to make an impression. According to the caption, her name was Karen Parker, a sixty-one-year-old retired social worker who offered first aid, food, and water to asylum seekers.

Karen lived in Boulevard, California, next door to Jacumba Hot Springs, California. I emailed the photographer and asked for her contact information, but he didn't know it. I then wrote to the Boulevard postmaster, enclosed a letter and a stamped envelope, and asked that it be forwarded it to her. Fewer than four hundred people live in Boulevard and I assumed the postmaster would know her, but I received no response. On a hunch, I called a church in Jacumba and asked the pastor about Karen. He knew her, gave me her phone number, and I called.

Her soft voice surprised me. I introduced myself and she said, Hello, Malcolm, as if we'd known each other for years. She wasn't surprised the Boulevard postmaster hadn't delivered my note. She had alienated more than a few people who opposed her work with asylum seekers.

A few weeks earlier she had received an odd phone call. *Tia*, a voice said, this is Hector. Spanish-speaking asylum seekers call Karen *tia*, Spanish for "aunt," so that didn't surprise her, but she didn't know anyone named Hector and wondered how he had gotten her number. There are a bunch of people who need help, need you, he said. How do you know me? Karen asked, but he wouldn't say. I'm aware of you, he told her. Don't tell anyone I called. Weird, Karen thought. She had seen men and women use their phones to shoot videos of asylum seekers and post them on Facebook, where trolls could harass them and anyone who helped them, like Karen. She wondered if

Hector was setting her up. For what, she didn't know. But he sounded very "sus," her slang for "suspect," and she got off the phone.

May I go out with you when you drive to the border? I asked.

Yes, she said, but only because you wrote me a letter. This is a small town and we're tired of reporters. If you were CNN, I'd tell you to fuck off.

———————

I had heard about asylum seekers crossing from Mexico into Jacumba Hot Springs months before I spoke to Karen.

The desert enclave of about six hundred souls is around seventy miles east of my San Diego home. Smugglers would guide men, women, and children through gaps in the border wall—an obsession of President Donald Trump's—that are less than half a mile from Main Street. The asylum seekers arranged makeshift camps until officers with Customs and Border Protection detained and processed them. Held for one or two days, many were released in San Diego at the Iris Street trolley station near Tijuana or at the airport on what the federal government called humanitarian parole. They had no place to charge cell phones or maintain hygiene. In addition, many of them were expected to appear in immigration courts in cities far from San Diego without the resources to travel. Others had been separated from family members during the detention process and didn't know how to find them.

In 2020, the federal government launched the CBP One app as a portal to various Customs and Border Protection services. Asylum seekers were required to answer questions on the app to receive an appointment with the Border Patrol. However, the app proved problematic. A wide variety of people seek asylum and the app, which suffered from internet and connectivity issues, was offered in only a few languages. In addition, the app split up families by giving different appointment dates, and sometimes it canceled appointments without explanation. As a result, many asylum seekers crossed into the US outside of ports of entry instead of relying on flawed technology.

By the time I began reading about asylum seekers, patrols on the Mexican side of the border had slowed migrant crossings into Jacumba, but by spring 2024 the numbers had ticked back up again. In the first five months of the year, the Border Patrol recorded nearly 152,000 migrant apprehensions in its San Diego sector, a 72 percent increase from fiscal year 2023, according to government data. In 2024, the San Diego sector became the second-busiest Border Patrol sector for illegal crossings, behind only the Tucson sector in Arizona.

As a freelance reporter, I had worked in Afghanistan. Several of my Afghan colleagues left the country for the US after the 2021 American withdrawal and the collapse of the government to the Taliban. Many more, however, remained behind because they had not been approved for a US visa. I tried to assist them, but I didn't have the government and military connections necessary to get them out. With each passing day, I felt the weight of my inability to help.

That experience made me sympathetic to asylum seekers. People fleeing for their lives can't stop, apply for visas, and wait months for a response in the very place they feel threatened. Under similar circumstances, I knew I would do as they had done: Cross into the US any way I could and apply for asylum.

———

I took Interstate 8 out of San Diego and arrived at Karen's apartment on Old Highway 80 at six o'clock on a Saturday morning. The empty highway stretched into the increased reddening of the sunrise, steamy heat rising off the pavement, the sky above as blue as glazed tile. A closed general store, Mountain Top Market & Gas, stood off the road, and the two fuel pumps cast long shadows into the pitted street. The traffic on the interstate sounded hollow and far off. Boulevard straddles the Tecate Divide, between the Laguna Mountains above and the desert below. From the highway, I could see the surrounding Laguna, In-Ko-Pah, and Sierra de Juárez mountains. The border was about seven miles south of here.

Karen met me at the end of her dirt-and-stone driveway and showed me where to park. My car bobbled over ruts and fissures. She wore clothes similar to what she was wear-

ing in her photo. Instead of a bandana, however, a black hat with a wide brim was perched
on her head. I like the brim, she said, grinning,
and ran a finger along its edge. She had just
gotten up, her voice scratchy from sleep. Her
two dogs, a nine-year-old Chihuahua and a
nine-month-old terrier mix scampered at her
feet. The terrier belonged to a litter of five
puppies a neighbor had discovered in a field.
Karen found homes for the mother and four
of the puppies. She kept the fifth and named
her Lilly.

  Her involvement with asylum seekers
began in May 2023 when she woke up one
morning to some men gathered around a
woman outside the general store. They spoke
Spanish but the woman didn't understand
them. Karen dressed and hurried outside. She
didn't speak Spanish but she had Google
Translate on her phone. She was certified in
CPR and first aid and worried the woman
might be hurt, but a quick exam didn't reveal
any injuries. A faded bracelet on the woman's
left wrist showed a name, Meryem. Turkish,
Karen realized, when she looked it up on her

phone. Together they used Google Translate to communicate. Meryem explained she had left Turkey in February 2023 after her house had collapsed from a 7.8-magnitude earthquake. More than 55,000 people had died. She was trying to reach family in Connecticut.

Facebook? Meryem asked Karen.

Karen tapped her Facebook app and Meryem found her homepage. She showed Karen photos of her two children—one nineteen, the other twenty. They had become separated after crossing the border near Jacumba. Using FaceTime, an app that allows users to make audio and video calls, she and Karen located her children in a camp not far from town. Karen drove her to them. Immigration and Customs Enforcement detained Meryem and her children for four weeks. After their release, they traveled to Connecticut. Karen never heard from them again.

Most people reach out afterward but then stop, Karen said. They go on with their lives. I don't blame them.

————

Karen shooed Lilly into a crate and we got in her white 2007 Ford SUV. Cases of water, boxes of fruit bars, ibuprofen bottles, gauze, and bandages bounced behind me as we followed Highway 80. Vacant houses stood off the street, faded white paint peeling from the weather-worn wood, and the empty windows revealed nothing within the dark interiors. Karen turned onto a dirt road that ran by a ranch. She slowed, crept along in low gear, the tires kicking gravel up into the fender wells. The guy who owns the ranch doesn't mind cars on this road as long as we drive slowly and don't disturb his horses, she said. A Great Pyrenees followed us behind a wire fence, prancing in the dirt and the stale heat while four seal-brown horses stood in a corral and watched. The SUV lurched to the rhythms imposed by deep holes and large rocks. Scrub puckered the sandy land and twisted limbs stretched out of the ground. Fencing sectioned off vast swaths of desolate terrain. A hawk circled above us and the emptiness we drove through. We rounded a curve and then climbed a hill. Ahead in the distance, emerging through the haze, I saw the rust-colored border wall jutting against the sky.

We turned onto a dirt road across from the wall and stopped. Through slats, I saw the Mexico National Guard on the other side standing by Jeeps. A few soldiers walked out of tents holding steaming cups of coffee. Karen waved.

I say hi to everyone so I don't look sus, even if they're on the other side of the wall, she said.

Karen was born in San Diego. She grew up in the rural town of Alpine, about forty minutes east of Boulevard. Her father and later a stepfather abandoned the family. With ten children to support, her mother bought an old switchboard and started a medical answering service. As she got older, Karen worked in hospitals auditing charts. As a social worker, she counseled addicts in King County, Washington. She married a Border Patrol officer (ironic, she admitted) and lived near the Canadian border. They had three children and later divorced. Grandchildren came along eventually, nine of them. During the pandemic,

Karen cared for her mother in Phoenix. After she died, Karen moved to Boulevard. She lived in her SUV until she found her apartment, a little shit box, she called it, for $1,200 a month.

My mother's mother came over here from Ireland when she was twelve, Karen said. She taught my mother how to survive, and my mother taught me how to survive. I learned how to take care of business.

———————

A Border Patrol Jeep stood on top of a dune, an officer watching us as we drove beside the wall. Karen recognized him. Months ago she had rolled into a migrant camp and met an Angolan woman who complained of a heart condition. This Border Patrol officer transported her to a hospital.

Nice guy, she said.

She drove toward him, pulled alongside and stopped.

Hi, she said.

The officer looked at her through his sunglasses.

See there's a strong Mexican guard presence. No asylum seekers here on our side, Karen said.

Maybe, the officer replied. Border Patrol picked up some bodies not far from here.

How many?

I don't know. I just heard them say they picked up the last of the bodies. You should try 177. Might be more bodies there.

You heard they have some? Karen asked.

No, but like you said, there's no one here.

Karen raised her hand goodbye and began driving. Bodies, she explained to me, referred to people. The first time she heard a Border Patrol officer say, I have a body, she thought someone had died. She considers the word dehumanizing. It's easier to be cruel, she said, if you see someone as a body instead of Meryem from Turkey. We found bodies. No face; no name. Like saying, we found rocks.

———

Around Jacumba, the asylum seekers are most often collected in four unofficial camps dubbed by locals as Willows, Moon Valley, O'Neil and San Diego Gas & Electric Tower 177. When a surge in migration started in the summer and fall of 2023, Border Patrol officers would tell hundreds of asylum seekers, including children, to stay in the camps or they would be deported. Conditions were dire. The asylum seekers had no food, shelter, or water. The days could be searingly hot and the nights frigidly cold. Asylum seekers waited hours or days before Border Patrol agents transferred them to detention facilities for processing.

In April 2024, a federal judge in Los Angeles ordered US border officials to process and move migrant children from camps throughout Southern California. At the center of the case were sites near San Diego and Jacumba.

In response to the ruling, the government released a statement: "[Customs and Border Patrol] will continue to transport vulnerable individuals and children encountered on the border to its facilities as quickly as possible."

However, families still wait hours, Karen told me. The Border Patrol officers want to catch bad guys, not transport women and children. Even when asylum seekers walk to the Boulevard detention facility, the Border Patrol, she said, sends them back to one of the camps—now called staging areas—to be picked up.

———————

Karen followed a gravel road to SDG&E Tower 177. The lone tower stood among huge boulders scattered at the base of a mountain, and abandoned black tarps hung over gaps in the rocks where asylum seekers had devised crude shelters the previous evening. Stripped manzanita trees lay against the tarps for additional protection. Karen broke her right arm here months earlier. Stepped out of her SUV, tripped, and fell. A Venezuelan nurse who had crossed the border and spent the night at 177 splinted her arm.

Karen inspected the remains of a smoldering campfire and found a charred MRE packet. *Asilo*, a handwritten sign read. Asylum. Wind lifted a mylar emergency blanket, ensnaring it in blue sage, and a disturbed snake inched out from beneath it. Karen peered inside a dumpster and saw torn bags of Cheetos, Doritos, and Twinkies. Junk food, salty, but good for hydration, she said. Discarded pants and tattered sneakers. Karen touched the pants. Damp. She wondered if the wearers had crossed a river or stream. She recalled one afternoon when she found four elderly women in wet clothes clustered in a group under a tree at this camp. They had been unable to keep up with their companions and sat in a circle like exhausted totems, waiting for the Border Patrol to pick them up.

———

We left 177, turned onto Ribbonwood Road and did not drive far before we saw them: A long, shimmering, broken line in the distance that became clearer as we approached, like field hands rising up through the heat and the powdery road dust, darkened by moments of shade. Up and over a rise, the scrape of roller luggage, women holding distraught babies against their chests, and the dazed men behind and around them, all of them shuffling forward, drifting under trees without pause until we pulled over in front of them and stopped.

They were walking toward Boulevard, presumably to turn themselves in to the Border Patrol. Karen looped a stethoscope around her neck, a prop to show she knows first aid, stepped out of the SUV and opened the hatch. Men and women gathered around us and then formed a silent line and waited as if we had all engaged in this routine before. I helped Karen distribute bottles of water and fruit bars. *A donde vas?* I asked people who I guessed came from Spanish-speaking countries. Where are you from? Peru, Colombia, Ecuador, came the replies. Other people who didn't speak Spanish knew enough English to answer with one word: China, Pakistan, Iraq. Their reasons varied. Gangs made life dangerous in Ecuador, Peru, and Colombia; in China, Pakistan, and Iraq, it was the economy and the secret police. And there was always government corruption.

Karen offered Band-Aids to people with blisters. She scanned the crowd for what she called solo kids—children, usually teenagers, unaccompanied by an adult. One month, she helped a twelve-year-old boy from Egypt. The boy's father had sent for him. She didn't ask about his mother. She may have died or stayed behind. Whatever the reason, Karen assumed it was probably something bad and didn't want to upset him. The boy followed her around until an older woman agreed to look after him. Solo kids try to blend in, Karen told me. They appear awkward and always look around; they gather in groups and smoke, ask where they can charge their phones and connect to Wi-Fi.

I continued distributing water until everyone had a bottle. Each person thanked me with quiet fortitude. They gripped my hands and bowed their heads. Using the Google translation app on her phone, Karen asked everyone to remain in one spot for the Border Patrol to pick them up. They won't let you in if you walk to the station, she said. I'll call and tell them where you are.

They smiled but ignored her and resumed walking. They had come too far to stop now. Some of them removed their jackets, tied them around their waists, covered their heads

17

from the sun, and moved on with a reserved grace in the unfiltered sunlight and soot and the tedium of their ongoing journey.

A Colombian man, his pregnant wife, and their two children, a boy and a girl, stopped and sat beneath a tree. The girl leaned on a pink roller suitcase with cat decals. A fence stood behind the tree and a sign on the gate read, Hidden Jewel Ranch. The twenty-acre estate hosted weddings, corporate and family events. A long road led into the ranch, winding out of sight. We stopped and gave the family food and water and crossword puzzles for the children. The woman told us she was eight months pregnant. With her permission, Karen pressed the diaphragm of her stethoscope against her swollen belly and listened to the fetal heartbeat. After a moment, she smiled. It's good, she said. *Muy bien.* The woman nodded. Her child will be a boy, Karen predicted. A boy, she typed into the translation app. She showed the woman her phone. *Un niño.* The woman smiled. We looked down the road at an ap-

proaching Border Patrol van, waited as it
slowed to a stop.

I've got a family here under a tree,
Karen told the agent, and a larger group, but
they're walking.

I'm full. The bodies I've got in here
slept outside last night. A group of forty.

I'm sure ours slept outside too. Can
you call ours in?

Yes.

Fair enough.

Glad to see you, the agent said. Do me
a favor.

Maybe, Karen said.

Tell whoever you see to stay where
they are.

I do. No one is staying.

I hear there's an autistic boy at Willows
Camp.

Willows?

Yeah.

I'll go there, Karen said.

It'll be six hours before I can get this
family here.

Karen nodded. She took off her sunglasses, faced the ground, pinched the top of her nose between her eyes, and sighed. She stood still, silently sorting through what was feasible and what was not, and then she put her glasses back on and tapped Google Translate on her phone.

OK, I'll tell them.

———

At Willows Camp, we parked near a scattered line of men and women resting in the angular shade provided by the wall. Sleeping bags lay open, and some people who were resting against backpacks on the rocky ground gave us a bewildered glance. A bulldog wandered through wagging its tail. Some people backed away, but one man gave it water and when it finished drinking he took what remained in the cup and poured it over his face, smudges of dirt turning to mud that trickled down his cheeks. The dog sat at his feet, panting.

The asylum seekers observed Karen opening the back of the SUV and then struggled to stand, hobbling forward, complaining of sore feet and bruised knees. Karen provided antiseptic spray and bandages. We asked them about the autistic boy, but no one knew of him.

Do you have water? a man asked me.

Yes.

I gave him a bottle.

I am from Sudan, he said.

He twisted off the cap. A dark beard wreathed his face. His tall, slim body swayed as he drank. He held a tattered shoulder pack, and his pants and T-shirt were torn. He noticed me looking at him and apologized for his appearance.

No worries, I said.

I presumed he had left Sudan because of the ongoing civil war. Government and rebel forces had been fighting since April 2023. More than eight million people had been displaced.

My name is Ahmed, he said. We crossed west of here.

He pointed behind us at a thin trail disappearing into scrub and cactus.

A Pakistani man asked Karen if she had anything for his pregnant wife's headache.

Karen rummaged through her boxes. The man's wife shuffled forward. Ahmed moved aside for her. Dried mud covered her white sweatshirt and black pants. Her wide, dark eyes looked glassy with fear, her soiled hair fell around her pale face, and she took fast, short breaths. Karen reached for a bottle of ibuprofen and a bottle of water. The woman watched as though she was caught in some inescapable realization and started to cry, slowly at first, until her face cracked with tears. Her husband stared at her with a helpless expression and extended a hesitant hand. Ahmed also watched her, his eyes watering, as if her distress belonged to him too. Karen opened her arms and the woman collapsed into her embrace and wept loudly. Her husband wiped away tears of his own. How many miles had they all traveled, through how many countries? I wondered. How many friends and family did they leave behind? The enormity of their decision to abandon their homes had finally caught up with them, as if this woman's headache, the ceaseless pain of it, had become a fissure that released all of their fears.

Oh, sweet girl, Karen whispered to her.

The woman pressed her face deeper into her chest and Karen massaged her shoulders, piled her hair on top of her head, and wiped her sweat-dampened neck with a water-soaked gauze pad.

It's going to be OK, she said.

Karen remembered meeting a Syrian man at this same camp months earlier. He had stared at her with a vacant gaze. He told her he had been held by ISIS for two years. He escaped and fled to Egypt. His family sent him money and he flew to Bolivia and then made his way on foot and by bus north toward Tijuana. How he wound up in Willows Camp, Karen didn't know. He had a compound fracture in his left foot that had healed on its own and he walked with a crooked gait. He spoke without blinking, his words hollow, his thoughts elsewhere. He saw Karen but didn't see her. Karen pointed to the tailgate of her SUV and suggested he sit. Together they ate tuna out of a can with a skinning knife. *You are here,* Karen told him. *This is my truck; this*

is the town of Jacumba. It is two in the afternoon. She gave him facts to ground him, to
bring him back from wherever his mind had
taken him.

Shh, Karen said to the woman now.
No one will hurt you.

She wiped tears from her cheeks. The
woman's husband put a hand on her back.
Ahmed wrapped an arm around the man's
shoulders. Dust rose in the distance. We heard
the sound of a vehicle and soon a white Border
Patrol van drove into view and stopped a few
feet from us. Karen slowly dropped her arms
from around the woman. Her husband stepped
in to hold her. An officer got out of the van.

We have three knee injuries and this
pregnant mom, Karen said. She's crying,
scared.

How bad are the injuries?

Cuts and scrapes. Not bad.

OK. I can take the pregnant mom and
any children traveling alone. Injured and
women and children are the priority. The rest
have to wait. I'll be back in an hour or so for
them.

Pregnant mom has a husband.

He can come. Any kids?

Not with them and no solo kids here that I've seen.

Karen motioned for the couple to walk with her to the van. Still crying, the woman followed her husband. The officer opened the van's sliding door. About forty asylum seekers squeezed together on bench seats stared out at us. Her husband got in and turned around for his wife. Karen held her hand and helped her in. The agent slammed the door shut.

What is happening? Ahmed asked me.

The Border Patrol will come back for the rest of you. They'll ask you questions, take some information, and then you will be released unless they decide to hold you longer.

Where?

I don't know.

Ahmed frowned. After a moment, he asked me if I had a WhatsApp number. I did, I told him, and gave it to him. He then offered me his.

Would you call someone for me? I have a sister. Her name is Maissa Salih. She lives in Chicago. She came here seven years ago and has a job in a hospital. I would call her but I have no signal here.

OK, I said.

He gave me her number.

Tell her I reached the United States.

———————

After we left Willows camp, Karen drove us back to her apartment. I thanked her for her time, got in my car, and reached San Diego about an hour later. I called Maissa, introduced myself, and told her I was a journalist. I had met Ahmed, I said, in a small town not far from San Diego.

Oh, she said and paused for a long time.

Hello? I said.

Thank you, she answered finally in a choked voice. I'm so happy. I don't know what to say.

It's OK.

She told me she had traveled to the US in 2017 when she was twenty to flee the fighting in Darfur. Her grandmother gave her money for a bus to Egypt. She paid smugglers to get her to Brasília, the capital of Brazil. From there she walked and took buses north until she reached Tijuana and crossed into California. She was held in the Otay Mesa Detention Center for three months before being released to a family friend in Fort Wayne, Indiana. She now rents a room in Chicago and works part time as a patient care technician. At night, she dreams of the fighting in Darfur. She hates to see people arguing, worries it will lead to violence. When she hears a car backfire, she thinks of bombs exploding.

I don't know how long the Border Patrol is going to hold Ahmed, I said. I presume he'll call you when he can.

OK, she said. Yes, yes. Thank you. Thank you so much.

Later that night, Karen called. I told her I had spoken to Maissa.

I wish her and Ahmed all the best, she said. I'm wondering about the Pakistani woman. I try not to get involved, but it's hard.

———————

Two days later, Maissa called me. A Border Patrol officer had contacted her. He asked if

Ahmed was her brother. Yes, she said. Are you willing to take responsibility for him? Yes, she replied. The officer said he would be released to her care. He would need to make an appointment with the Chicago Immigration Court. The officer did not say how he might reach Chicago.

That afternoon, Ahmed texted Maissa. The Border Patrol had dropped him off at the San Diego International Airport. He had nothing but the clothes he was wearing and his shoulder pack. Maissa called me again. She wanted to fly Ahmed to Chicago but only had one hundred dollars. I got online and bought him a one-way ticket to Chicago on United Airlines. A cynic would say she played me. Maybe, but I don't think so. I thought of my Afghan colleagues and wished I had been able to help them as easily.

Ahmed's flight didn't leave until 10 the next morning. I called him on WhatsApp and offered to pick him up and let him stay the night with me, but he was afraid to leave the airport. He worried he wouldn't be allowed back in. He told me had traveled from Sudan to Cameroon, Chad, Morocco, Spain, Bolivia, Colombia, Panama, Nicaragua, Honduras, Guatemala, and Mexico by plane, bus, and foot. He had paid a coyote in Tijuana to lead him into California. He had sold twenty-five cows on his family's farm and had gone through Maissa's savings to get here. He would not risk a mistake now. He would remain at the airport.

———

Ahmed and I arranged to meet. I made four cheese-and-tomato sandwiches for him and then drove to a supermarket. The crowded parking lot teemed with families, and a little girl skipped ahead of me as I entered the store, and I stood aside for her parents to catch up to her. I bought green grapes and a bag of tortilla chips. I also withdrew cash from an ATM. A driver waited for my parking spot as I got back in my car and left. Twenty minutes later, I reached the airport and maneuvered through traffic toward the curb where I saw Ahmed waiting for me. He wore a brown, faux-leather jacket, a pink shirt, and blue jeans that the Border Patrol had given him. He smiled as if he didn't have any concerns. I gave him the food and money.

Let me know when you reach Chicago.

Yes, he said.

————

The next morning, Ahmed called to say he was boarding the plane. That evening, Maissa sent a photograph to my phone. It showed her and Ahmed sitting at a picnic table. The branches of an elm hovered above them. Maissa was leaning forward, arms crossed, grinning. She wore a black head scarf and a light blue body length gown. Ahmed sat beside her in a striped T-shirt, his right arm extended to snap the photo with her phone, a bemused, weary expression on his face.

What he had accomplished had been done by generations of asylum seekers. He had traveled thousands of miles to reach the United States, then spent his first nights detained by the Border Patrol and then at an airport. But now he had reached his destination; he had reunited with Maissa, who had experienced similar travails in her journey. He was free to pursue the things that would fulfill him.

An immigration judge would determine his future, but for now he could stop running.

Ahmed is home, Maissa texted.

––––––––––

I telephoned Karen and told her Ahmed had reached Chicago. Great, she said, fantastic! Just before I called, she told me, she had heard a high-pitched whining like nails on a chalkboard. The noise emanated from a cordless reciprocating saw, a tool that can cut through metal and retails at hardware stores for about one hundred dollars. Smugglers use them to open gaps in the wall large enough for people to squeeze through. Karen imagined asylum seekers crawling into Jacumba, running in the dark. Some of them may be criminals—she wasn't naive—but not most of them. The Pakistani woman certainly wasn't. Neither was Ahmed. They were brave, lost souls who sought a better life. Why was that a crime?

She doubted I'd hear from Ahmed again. Our chance encounter had served its purpose. Face forward. Get on with life. She wished him all the best.